Mud Pie

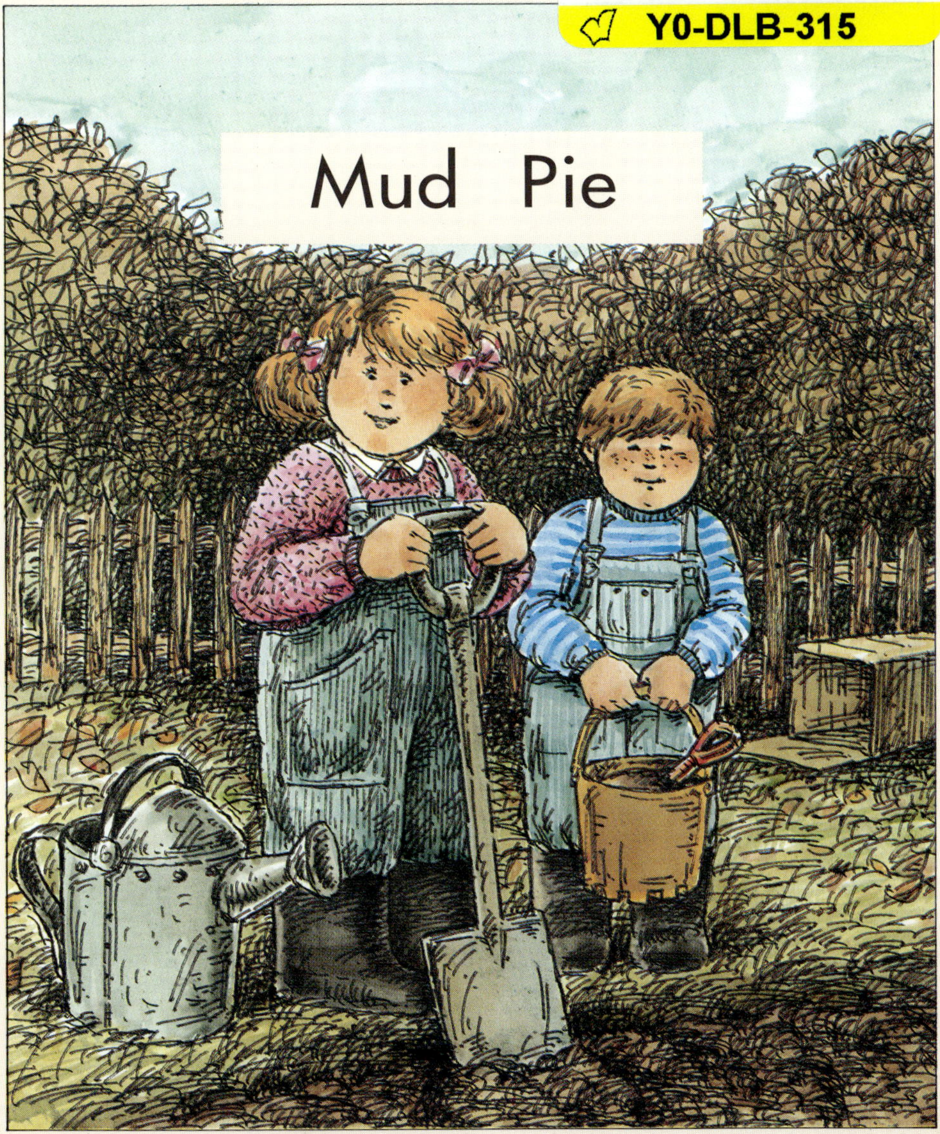

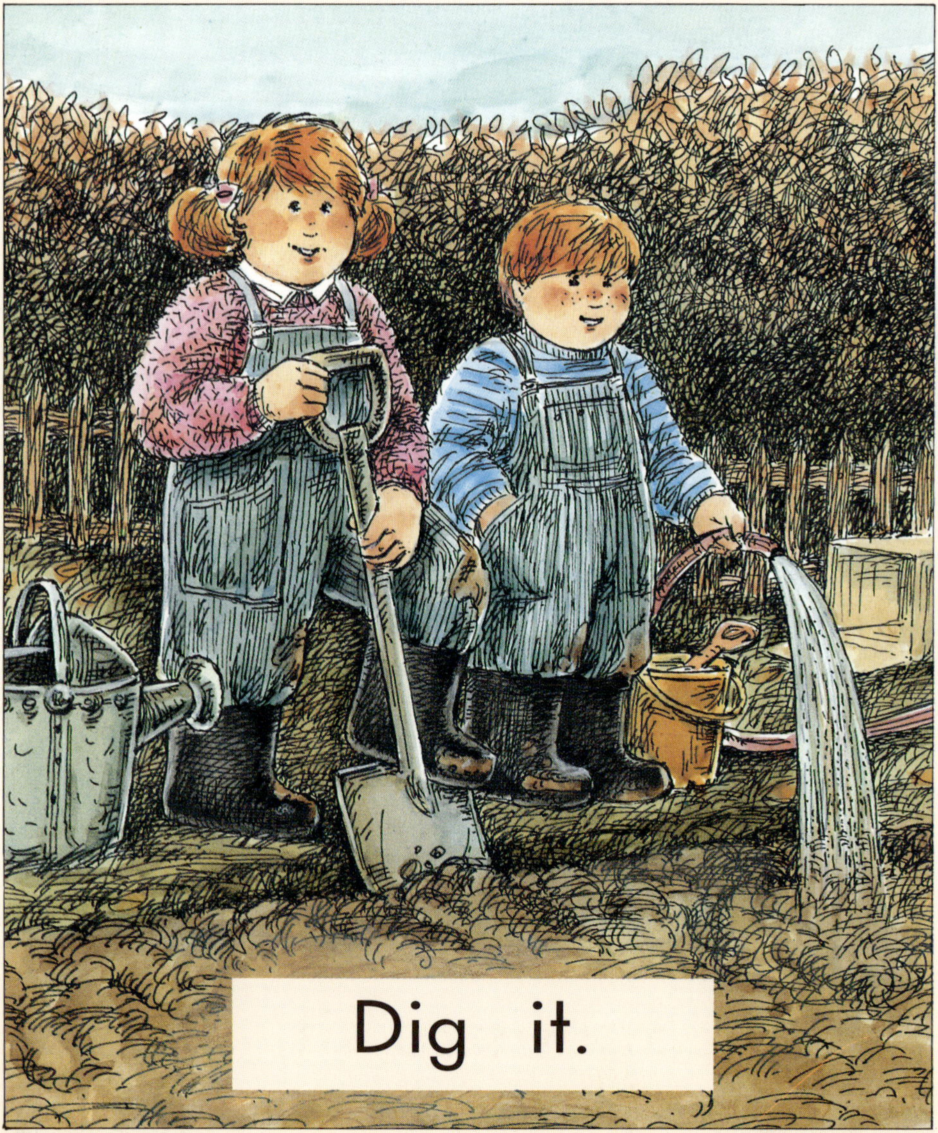

Dig it.

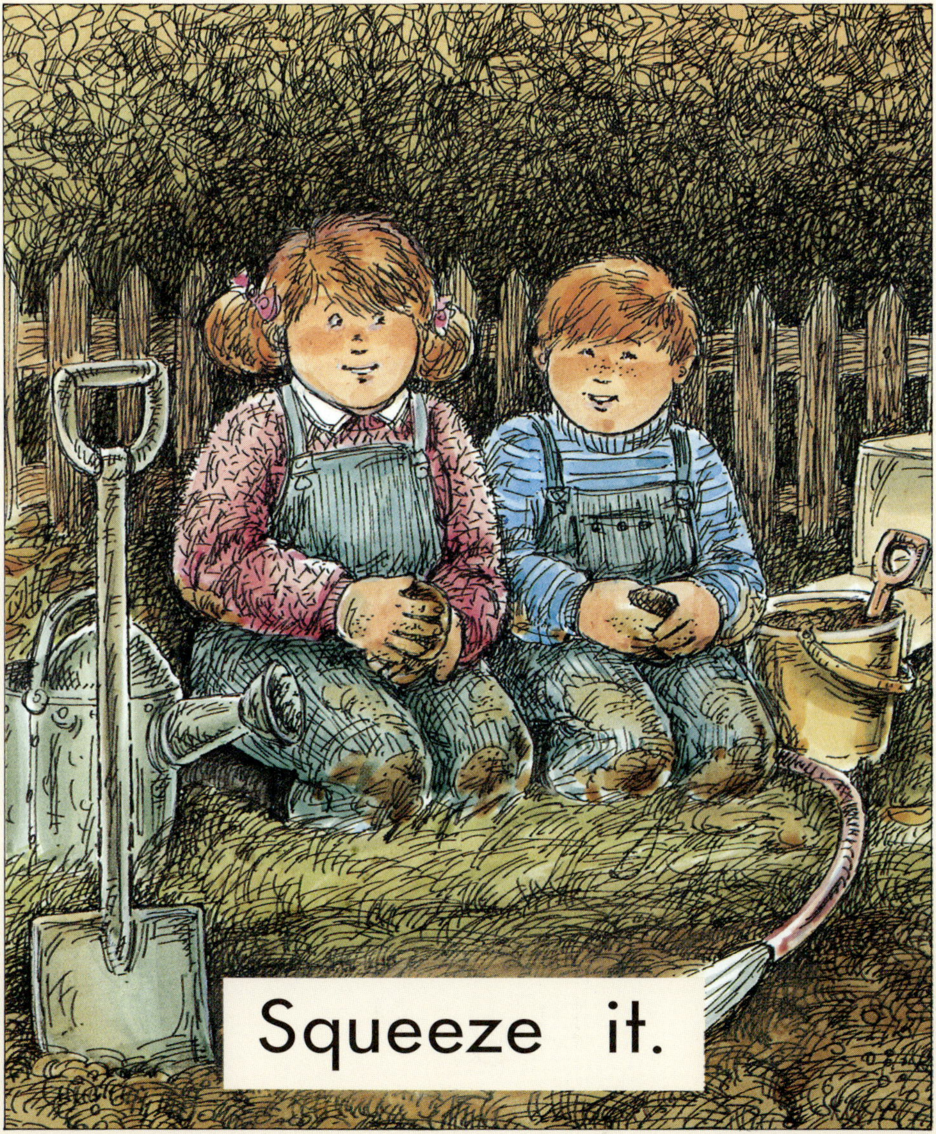

Squeeze it.

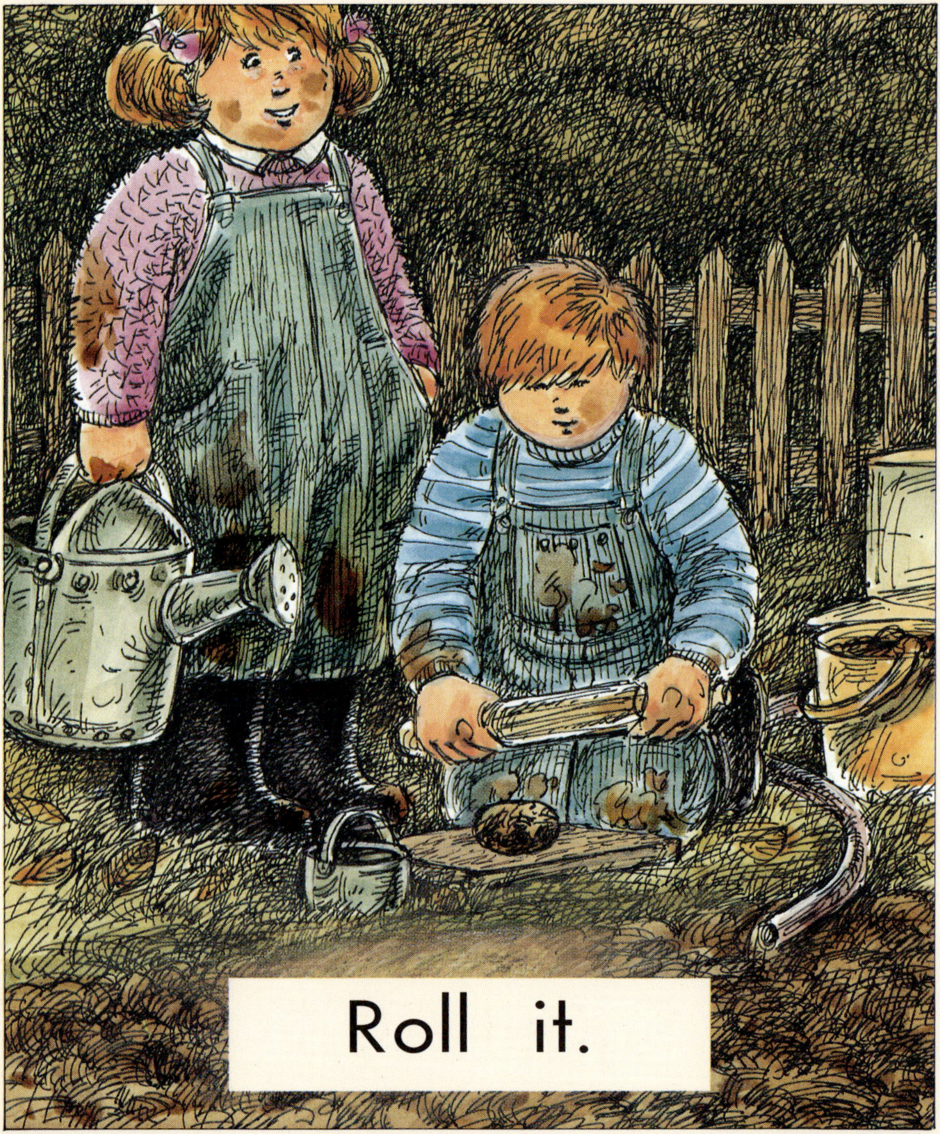

Roll it.

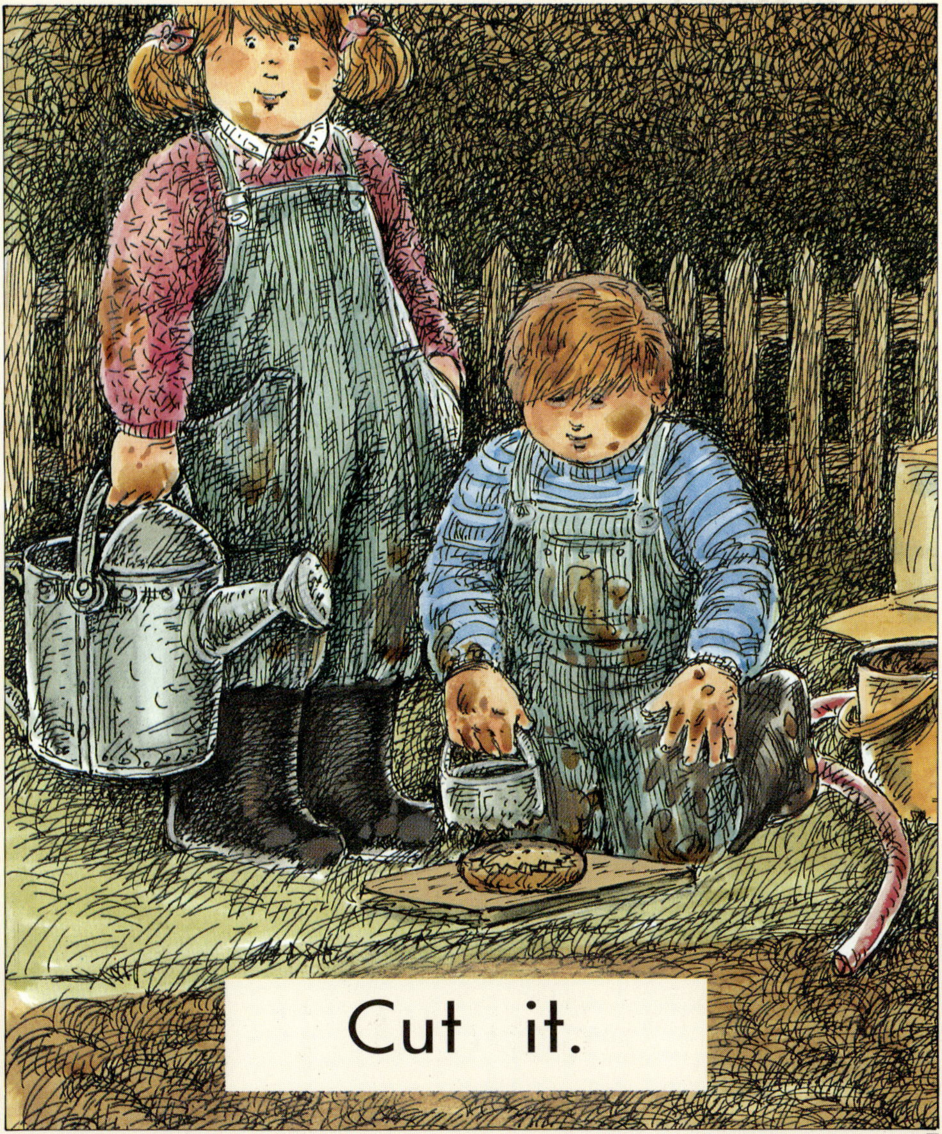

Cut it.

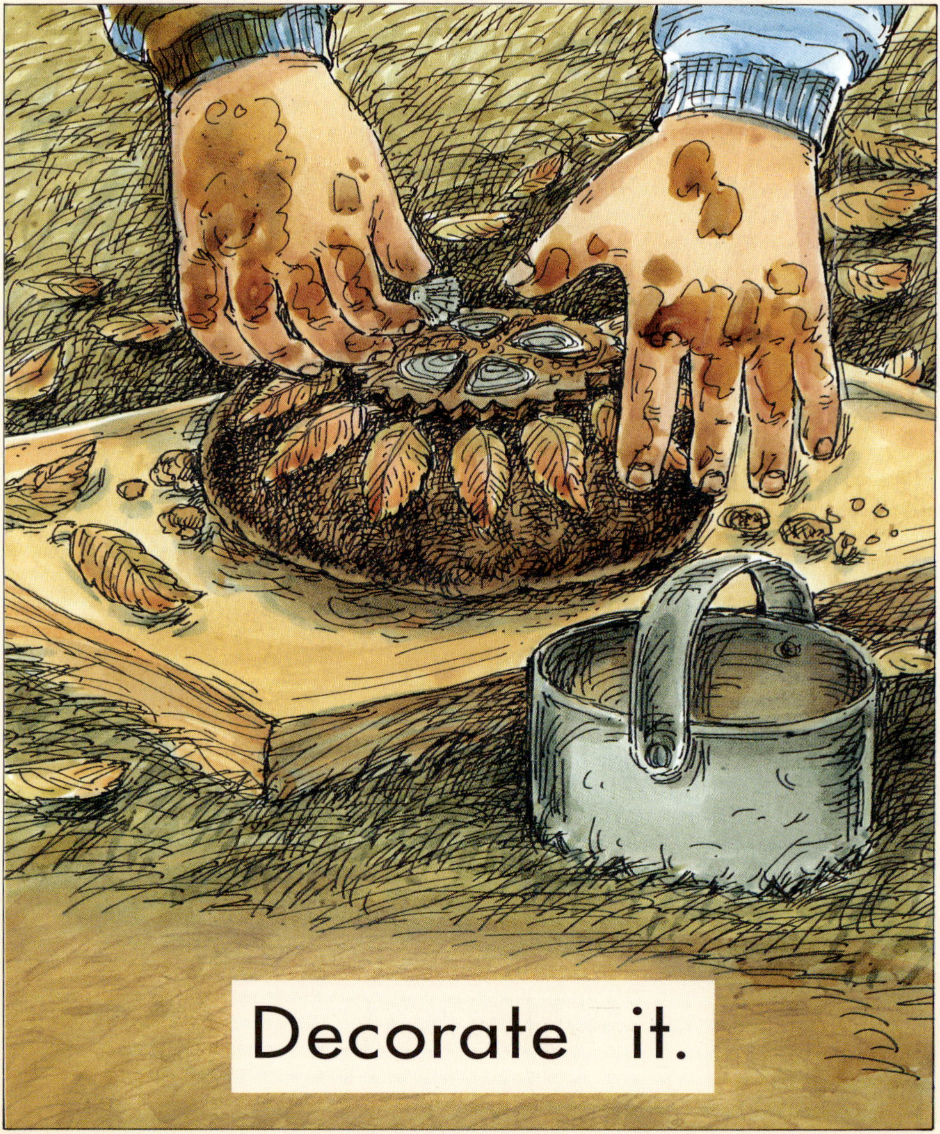

Decorate it.

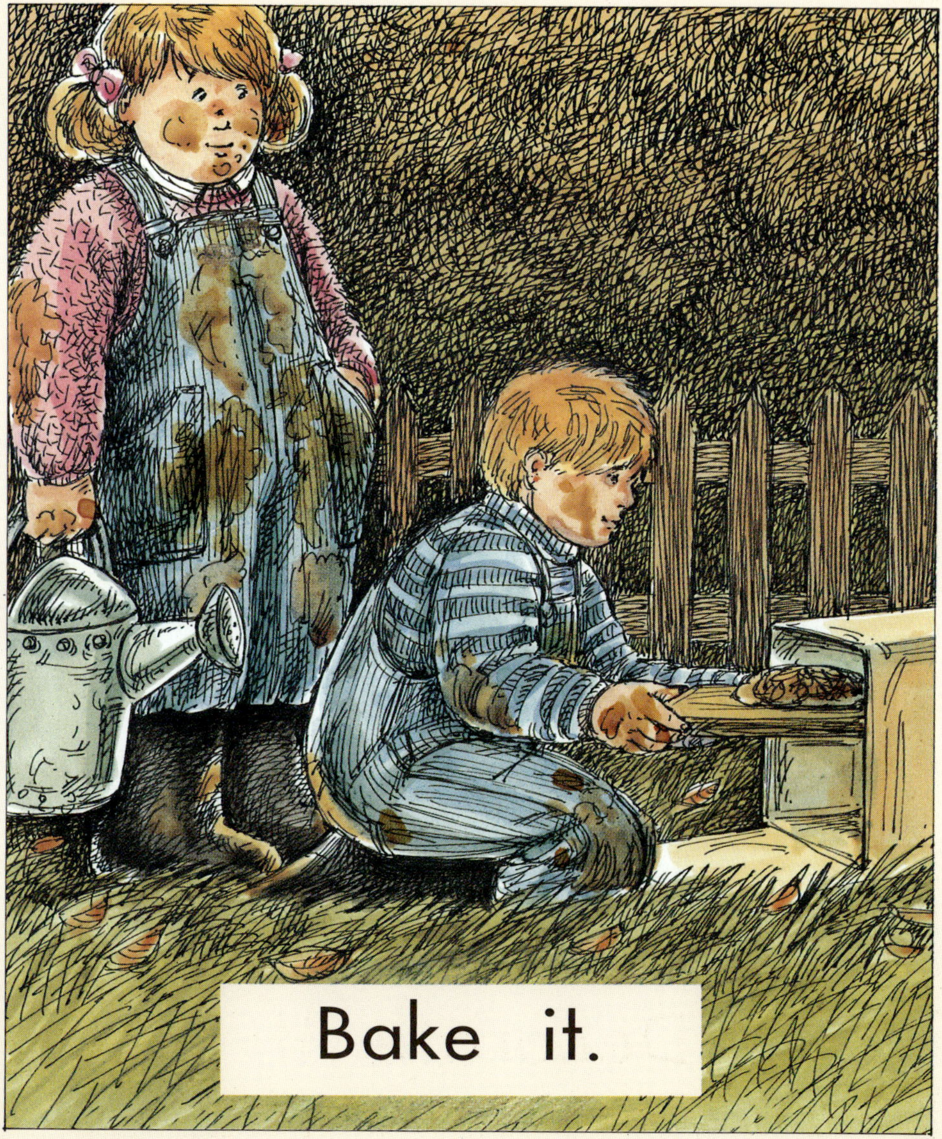

Bake it.

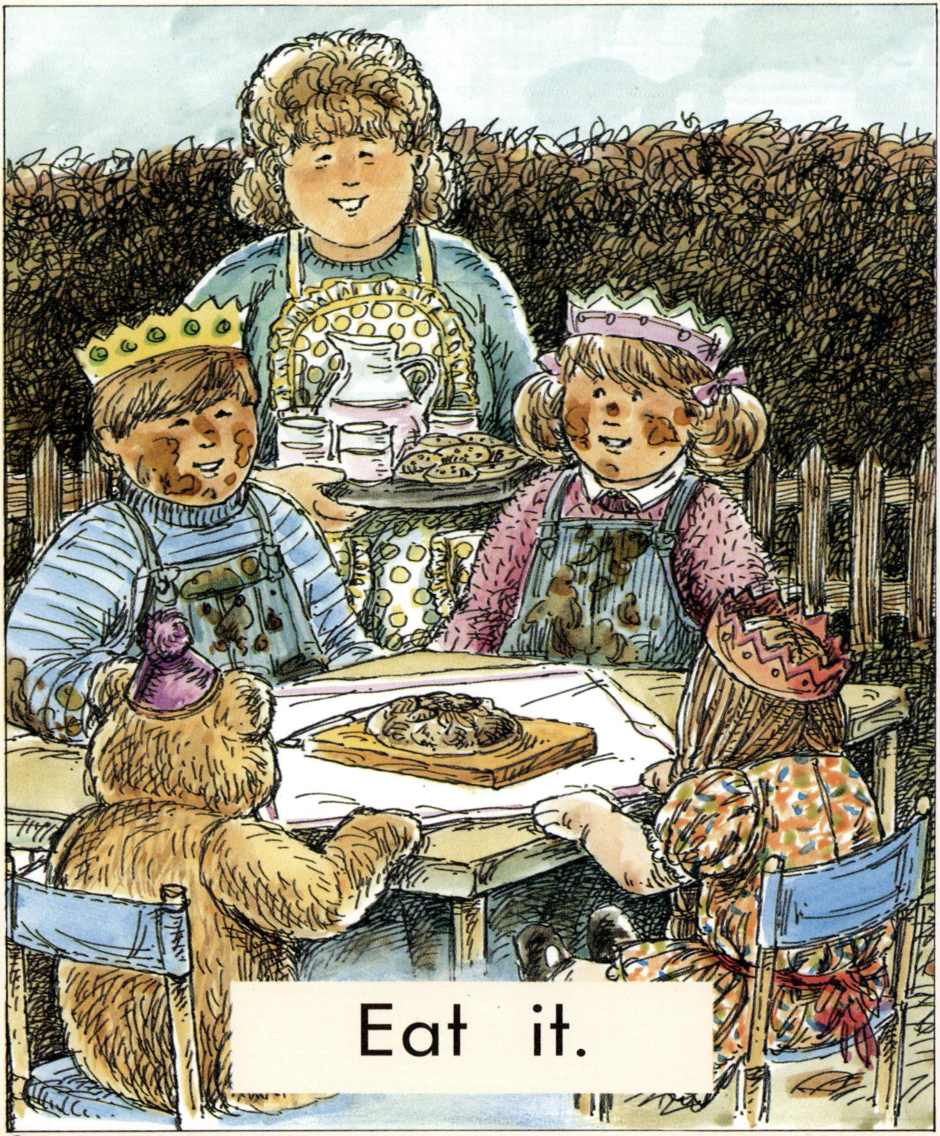

Eat it.